SUM~~MARY~~

&ANALYSIS

OF

THE
CONFIDENCE GAP

A GUIDE TO OVERCOMING FEAR & SELF-DOUBT

A GUIDE TO THE BOOK
BY RUSS HARRIS

TABLE OF CONTENTS

SYNOPSIS... 4

THE TEN RULES FOR CONFIDENCE 5

KEY THEMES & TAKEAWAYS 8

EDITORIAL REVIEW 34

BACKGROUND ON AUTHOR... 37

SYNOPSIS

Russ Harris lays out the key to self-development in his book, *The Confidence Gap*. Using the basic premises of the mindfulness movement, this step-by-step guide to a happier, healthier mentality marches through relatable acronyms, ten rules to bring it full circle, and plenty of disclosure on the author's imperfect practice of his own suggestions.

It begins with a detailed analysis of confidence itself—why it is an elusive quality to achieve, what it looks like, and how to get it. Questions (or personal analysis prompts) are provided to fuel enthusiastic participation, illuminating the reader with regards to their own deeply-ingrained views and values. These questions are then linked to finding confidence, motivation and a 'transformed' perspective of fear.

The guide goes on to address the myths of confidence, solutions to common issues, and a few acronyms to remember when using the Acceptance and Commitment Training (ACT) techniques. The confidence-finding rules include simple, but significant reminders for taking action despite feelings, conquering the relationship we have with our fears, accepting our thoughts, tuning in to our values, and engaging fully in the life we live one task at a time.

His explanation on values and goals follows with a prompt to eke out a "life-change list," which explores areas, qualities and actions you anticipate will be different in the face of achieving genuine confidence. Encouragement, tips and troubleshooting scenarios provide a final push into a life of confidence, success and commitment to action.

THE TEN RULES FOR CONFIDENCE

Finding genuine confidence requires several key moves, including being committed to taking action, being in touch with your value system, and being mindful, or fully aware of your inner thoughts and feelings; and how these affect you on a physical, mental and spiritual level.

"When mindfulness, values, and committed action come together, they give rise to psychological flexibility, the ability to take effective action, guided by values, with awareness, openness, and focus" (Harris, Introduction).

The Confidence Gap cites ten rules for true confidence. The rules are to be used as a guide with a flexible attitude to personalizing, or even dropping rules where relevant.

THE TEN RULES ARE:

1. The actions of confidence come first; the feelings of confidence may come later.

But if they don't, at least you have taken action: the best way to "act with confidence."

2. Genuine confidence is not the absence of fear but a transformed relationship with fear

This includes a different perspective on what fear can do for, rather than to you.

3. Negative thoughts are normal. Don't fight them; defuse them.

4. Self-acceptance trumps self-esteem.

We should work on accepting our reactions, our mind's "radio commentary" and our difficult emotions, rather than reacting with frustration, or trying to avoid or eradicate them.

5. True success is living by your values.

Our measurement of success should be based how well we live out our values and beliefs, not on the goals we achieve. There are always more goals to be reached, but values are permanent. Values are also what we draw confidence and motivation from to be able to pursue our goals.

6. Hold your values lightly but pursue them vigorously.

In other words, know that values underlie our decisions and directions and set goals that are in line with your value system, but don't berate yourself when you fail to embody a value—such not showing courage in a certain situation.

7. Don't obsess about the outcome; get passionate about the process. In other words, enjoy the journey

8. Don't fight your fear: allow it, befriend it, and channel it.

Fear is compared to a wild stallion who arrives on your land, full of potential. With the right approach and patient acceptance, there is power to be harnessed from it.

9. Failure hurts—but if we're willing to learn, it's a wonderful teacher.

Failure is turned into success when we are open to correction, gather positive aspects of the experience, and don't compromise on our values throughout the process.

10. The key to peak performance is total engagement in the task.

No matter the level of anxiety we harbor, confident performance depends on our ability to focus fully on the task at hand.

KEY THEMES & TAKEAWAYS

MINDFULNESS

The practice of mindfulness relies largely on acceptance and engagement. Harris employs the techniques of *Acceptance and Commitment Training* (ACT). ACT is the brainchild of Steven Hayes, PhD (and writer of the preface), a professor of psychology at the University of Nevada. ACT encourages a mindful approach to life, encouraging us to put committed action into full use without eradicating or avoiding the thoughts or feelings a person EMITS (emotions, memories, images, thoughts, sensations).

Through constant reminders to notice what your mind is doing or thinking or saying, *The Confidence Gap* is underpinned by the framework of mindfulness and meditation. It wills us to notice, to observe, and to hopefully accept the circus within. It also assures us that a range of reactions and thought patterns is normal, natural, human, and inevitable. The key is to notice is but not to change it, no matter whether it is "*being positive or negative, encouraging or discouraging, enthusiastic or doubtful*" (Harris, Ch. 1).

KEY TAKEAWAY: COMMITTED ACTION RESULTS IN INSTANT SUCCESS

Mindful action with full engagement in the task and staying true to your values is guaranteed to result in success. If we commit to the task, and become fully engaged in its every detail, we will see positive results even when it is long and difficult. Even if the goal isn't achieved as envisioned, its foundational value is honored—acting with integrity or courage, for example—which makes it a successful undertaking.

"The trick is to embark on your adventure and travel mindfully, guided by your values, even if you don't feel the way you'd prefer to. This would be an example of acting with confidence" (Harris, Ch. 17).

Key Takeaway: The mind's best quality may be its worst enemy

It is natural for the mind to analyze each situation (including thoughts and actions) and to give feedback and criticism, and to play devil's advocate.

This relentless inner voice, likened to a radio continuously broadcasting in the background, tends to linger on knee-jerk judgements and worst-case scenarios. "It's always got an opinion, an idea, a prediction, a judgement, a criticism, a comparison, or a complaint" (Harris, Ch. 6). This is highly unhelpful in a situation where you are trying to stay motivated, be positive, or receive encouragement to tackle some grueling endeavor. Consequently, mindfulness techniques can help you to use the mind's insatiable diatribe to your advantage: learning to accept its rant without being hooked into the emotions and harness the helpful bits and pieces it provides.

The radio analogy also provides a technique to 'unhook' from the distraction of the inner voice—to start the process of defusion. Once we notice the "radio" broadcast and specify the theme with familiar names or references, it becomes easier to imagine the radio blasting through a speaker, letting us hear it and observe it, but not internalize its message.

KEY TAKEAWAY: ACTING MINDFULLY OPENS UP ROOM FOR SELF-DEVELOPMENT AND PERSISTENCE

Once trained in the art of mindful engagement, you can accept and make room for emotions, memories, images, thoughts and sensations (EMITS). By responding only to those deemed worthy of our energy and time, we bypass inefficient efforts to control or to stay clear of difficult feelings and thoughts. The extra time and energy left is then available to be invested into worthwhile tasks, like achieving goals and purposefully living out your values.

Persistence, or dedication to succeeding in life, follows continuous self-development and a discovery of genuine confidence. You develop the capacity to succeed by being mindful of your values. Notice how you feel about what you are doing and thinking. Focus wholeheartedly on living those values out, no matter the obstacles or outcome. This way of life is bound to develop confidence as you learn to trust yourself and believe in your abilities over and over again.

KEY TAKEAWAY: DEFUSION, EXPANSION AND ENGAGEMENT ARE THREE OF THE MOST RELEVANT MINDFULNESS TECHNIQUES TO DEVELOPING GENUINE CONFIDENCE.

Mindfulness techniques begin with the simple task of 'noticing what your mind is telling you.' Focus on you thoughts, the words and images, and the sensations they evoke in your body: physical reactions, posture, vibrations. What is your mind saying? What is your body doing? How are your emotions changing? Once we have taken notice, the next steps are defusion, expansion, and engagement with these thoughts and feelings.

Defusion

Defusion—separating from thoughts instead of allowing them to influence your actions—helps to still the incessant waves of "worse-case scenario" monologue present in the mind. The thoughts and feelings will come anyway. Our response to it does not need to be an automatic reaction. This way of disconnecting from thoughts and emotions allows us to be present in each moment and take decisive action when the need arises.

Separating from your thoughts and feelings can be a tricky process, however, especially when it is personal, often negative feedback. The third rule is: *"Negative thoughts are normal. Don't fight them; defuse them"* (Harris, Ch. 5).

Easy defusion techniques mentioned are: "I'm having the thought that…", singing your thoughts to a well-known tune or using silly voices to repeat them out loud, pretending to view the images or words on a black and white computer screen (and then adding splashes of color or light), "thanking" our mind for its input, and using visual distractions (like "if your hands were your thoughts…").

"Keep in mind, these techniques are like training wheels on a bicycle. You won't have to go for the rest of your life singing your thoughts to "Happy Birthday" or hearing them in the voice of Homer Simpson. This is just a convenient place to start" (Harris, Ch. 5).

Expansion

Expansion—or 'making space' for "emotions, sensations, and feelings"—is the ability to let things be without being caught up in the backwash. We recognize it but aren't tied to it. We begin to understand the source from an observer's perspective rather than as an active participant.

Difficult emotions or thoughts have the power to "hook" us on to all sorts of troublesome tangents, derailing effective action at the best of times. Expansion helps to give the problem its proper perspective in our reality, so once we sit back and think about our difficult emotion or fear, allowing it to come and go freely, and "making space" for it as part of our reality, it loses its sting.

Once expansion skills are second nature, however, it becomes possible to handle difficulties on the go. To not simply tolerate them, but fully accept them as part of the experience.

Chapter 15 lists the following pitfalls to be aware of when expansion techniques:

· Attempting to stop or remove the feeling.

· Falsely believing you have conquered it when it has only faded into the background to reappear later (with vengeance).

· Paying too much attention to fear-mongering, critical comments and self-loathing instead of defusing or 'unhooking.'

· Tolerating the feeling instead of moving towards true acceptance (no gritted teeth allowed, please).

· Losing focus on the goal (which is to make space for the feeling in order to succeed in values-based living).

Engagement

Engagement—being "psychologically present" or aware of the moment—allows maximum experience in any of life's domains. Clear focus on the task at hand ensures complete enjoyment of it, and performance excellence, as you put away distractions and give it your all. Being engaged thus cultivates an openness—an endless sense of wonder and active involvement in each moment—be it in love, work, health or play.

Mindfulness means noticing. It is paying attention to every part of the present moment, both internally and externally. It is a flexible approach to life, being able to build awareness of the physical, emotional and spiritual aspects of any given point in time with the intention to see it, hear it, feel it, examine it, and let it play out unhindered. Thus, engagement is essential for excellence, peak performance, maximum enjoyment and lasting contentment.

Practice and Commitment

The message is clear: confidence is a skill and it can be developed through patient perseverance. Committed action aims to bring a true confidence to the forefront, independent of feelings, shortcomings or circumstances.

Key Takeaway: Practice is essential to the effective development of any skill

Confidence requires practice like any other skill. To master it requires practice, experience and even coaching or mentoring. There is no satisfaction in picking up an instrument when you have neither the skills nor the inclination to use it as it was meant to be handled. There will be no beautiful music or magical composition where there is no cultivation of skills through dedicated practice.

The aforementioned mindfulness techniques for defusion, expansion, and engagement, for example, are foundational to the development of healthy and lasting confidence. But it takes practice and hard commitment to master the skill over a lifetime. If we rely on ourselves, or trust ourselves, over and over again as we commit to taking an action and do it, despite fear or other emotional obstacles, we develop confidence. We know we can do it because we have done it before, again and again.

A healthy attitude is that there is always room for improvement, no matter how confident you think you may be.

The confidence cycle is key here: practice the skill, apply it well, assess its effectiveness and be open to modifying action where necessary. *"As Tiger Woods puts it, 'No matter how good you get, you can always get better—and that's the exciting part'"* (Ch. 11).

KEY TAKEAWAY: PRACTICE IS NOT ALWAYS ENOUGH.

Like any acquired skill, true confidence may not be adequately developed through practicing a handful of simple techniques. There are times where we need outside assistance like a coach or a mentor, for example. There may also be some other difficulties you will need to work through, like deep-seated anxiety, mental health issues, or learning barriers.

As any professional sportsman will agree, natural ability can only take you so far. Practice is essential, but to reach past personal limitations you may need to be aware of blind spots or shown a more effective technique by an objective ally. Be open to accepting help with grace.

"While practice is vitally important, it's not enough; we also need to apply our skills effectively. That means we need to make room for our feelings, unhook ourselves from our thoughts, and engage fully in the task at hand" (Harris, Ch. 1).

KEY TAKEAWAY: COMMITMENT IS A CULTIVATED HABIT AND IT SAVED JOE SIMPSON'S LIFE.

The task-focused attention of Joe Simpson is a viable source of inspiration in the confidence game. His commitment to his task was a death-defying mental feat not many would be able to replicate.

Left for dead by his fellow adventurers in an icy wasteland, Joe was faced with certain death, alone and afraid. He documents this in his book *Touching the Void*. Chapter 17 lists six lessons from Joe Simpson's experience which are related to committed action:

1. When we face major challenges in life, if we move forward guided by our values, we will feel a sense of meaning and purpose.

2. Even when we think a goal is impossible, we can still keep moving toward it.

3. As long as we keep moving forward, every little step counts.

4. Moving in a meaningful direction often gives rise to uncomfortable thoughts, feelings and sensations.

5. If we wish to act effectively in challenging situations, we need to engage fully in what we are doing.

6. At times, we will all give up, as Joe Simpson did each time he was ready to die. Commitment doesn't mean we never give up or go off track. It means we come back and keep going after we falter.

BALANCE

A healthy balance in life has been the subject of many psychological avenues. Balance proves more of an ideal than a goal, as our equilibrium changes with each new phase of life. Whether in love, work or play, the idea is to remain engaged and encouraged by the smallest bouts of progress. General well-being (including physical and mental health) is as important as successful achievement and service.

"Appreciate your commitment, appreciate everything you did that worked reasonably well, appreciate your own willingness to take a risk, and especially appreciate anything you did that was an improvement on last time, no matter how small it may be. This is essential, not only for self-acceptance but also for ongoing energy, drive, and enthusiasm" (Harris, Ch. 22).

KEY TAKEAWAY: BEHAVIOR MUST ALIGN WITH EXPECTATIONS

When our reality falls short of our expectations, problems arise. It is expectations which create doubt, disappointment and fear. Excessive expectations are especially dangerous in the realm of confidence-building.

But expectations are natural and are a sure way to aim for higher and better places in life. Dreams and hopes build nations. The key is to align expectations with behavior, making sure your expectations are achievable, or improving performance over time to match the expectation. It also requires flexibility and moderation. Stick with 'workable' resources and situations, which help the cause and encourage excellence.

KEY TAKEAWAY: OVER-COMMITMENT RESULTS IN BURNOUT AND FRUSTRATION

Wherever there is ambition, there is over-commitment. Burnout is often the result of this over-commitment to goals which do not align with your values. Being in touch with our values will counteract this tendency as we show courage and commitment to achieving goals in line with our deepest dreams and desires.

KEY TAKEAWAY: REALITY GAPS ARE AN OPPORTUNITY TO REASSESS THE SITUATION

The confidence gap is where reality falls short of expectation and we are trapped in a cycle of "waiting" to act until we "feel more confident." This reality gap applies to other areas, such as motivation, and presents a rare opportunity to change our attitudes. Once we realize that committed action trumps the "waiting," and is usually accompanied by fear, there are suddenly no more excuses as to why we aren't doing something valuable with our precious time.

"Mark Twain said, 'Twenty years from now you will be more disappointed by the things that you didn't do than by the ones you did do.' So throw off the bowlines. Sail away from the safe harbor. Catch the trade winds in your sails. Explore Dream. Discover" (Harris, Ch. 17).

Key Takeaway: Moderation is a magnificent tool for contentment

The last question of balance involves a serious look at whether excellence is better than moderation in various life goals. It is healthy to have one or two areas for which we pursue perfection, but in most other domains, we may be more content just to be competent. Being competent, rather than excellent, can still lead to "a balanced and rewarding life" (Ch. 22).

Self-Development

As he relates a "successful celebrities" lineup, Harris concludes that all of them have the common character traits of persistence and self-development. None of them settled for less than they could be or do. None of them gave up (although many of them quit along the way, but always managed to pull themselves back "on to the horse"). The people mentioned range from survival heroes, like Joe Simpson, to world leaders, like Nelson Mandela, and sports stars, like Tiger Woods.

Key Takeaway: It is necessary to be kind to yourself.

Failure is inevitable, but true failure is giving up entirely. In his admiration of Joe Simpson of *Touching the Void*, the man who dragged his broken body across frozen wastelands and survived, Harris unveils the secret to persistence: self-appreciation, self-encouragement and being open to giving yourself second (and third and fourth) chances to succeed. The mind is already hypercritical of each and every action, decision or scenario we face—be kinder to yourself and see how much difference it makes.

We are reminded that the mind has a tendency to over criticize its every move. Harsh self-judgement is one of the five key reasons for low confidence. Being kinder to yourself remedies this in a meaningful effort to defuse with the ideas that you are "no good" or "don't know what you are doing."

Key Takeaway: Growth means change.

Growth is necessary in every aspect of life. We see it in the natural order where it is a choice between death or adaptation. Growth is painful, however, but worth it for the stunning reward of genuine confidence, among other qualities.

Growth also negates boredom as it helps us to develop our mindfulness effectively. Paying attention to life's many details with the apt wonder of a wide-eyed child disallows boredom, which stems from thoughtless distraction and mundane disillusionment.

Key Takeaway: Self-Doubt is normal and natural.

There are continuous reminders that self-doubt is a natural phenomenon. It is inherent in human nature to question yourself, to rue your decisions and to wonder whether it was all worth it. Self-doubt is normal. Self-doubt is also inevitable. They key is to use it to your advantage, taking the good with you into future endeavors and throwing out the rubbish.

Key Takeaway: Values-based living paves the way for self-development

The inspirational people dotted throughout the book share the pursuit of personal values such as persistence and self-development. The paths to reach these qualities differed tremendously, with different action plans, experiences, aims and hopes. They all continued despite difficulties, never taking their eyes off the ball for long. They all focused on improvement in their field, honing skills, seeking mentorship and accepting correction when it counted.

For each one, the values they held dear determined their steps and their direction, as well as the attitude with which they approached the obstacle-fraught journey. Living true to your values is the definition of success, no matter whether specific goals are achieved along the way. It is living with integrity and that cannot lead to regrets.

KEY TAKEAWAY: WORRY IS A NATURAL PART OF LIFE, BUT IT DOES NOT HAVE TO RUN YOUR LIFE.

A large section of chapter ten deals with worry. It is a natural part of life, not a sign of weakness. It is proof of concern and commitment. Worry is bound to crop up in even the most balanced mind, but again, the mindfulness techniques mentioned should help you to notice, name and neutralize the difficulties.

The problems occur when we do not defuse from the worry, when we internalize it and mull over it, letting it drag us down and derail our self-development. The negative effects of worry include stress, reduced motivation and impaired capacity for action. It also leaves us distracted and looking for answers in the wrong places.

Avoidance mode is a by-product of our preoccupation with worry. People are used to opting out at the first sign of discomfort, even when it is in pursuit of a highly desired outcome. Interestingly, the book mentions R. Rich and D.F Woolever in their work which showed that similar levels of anxiety in academic performance produced vastly different performance from the candidates. Their conclusion was that the difference was the result of task-focused engagement in the exam, not the anxiety present.

Key Takeaway: Low confidence is not indicative of capability

There are five main reasons listed for low confidence, including harsh self-judgment and excessive expectations. The effect of fear on confidence is also an example of perception versus reality. Although the reason for low confidence may be a low level of experience or skills to complete the task, this is often not the case, or it can easily be remedied by gaining the training or mentoring required.

Harris lays out the example of one of his patients who had trouble in social situations. The patient did not have a lack of social skills, only low confidence as a result of severe self-judgement. Once she took it easier on herself and boosted her confidence, her existing social skills could flourish in previously terrifying situations. Her low confidence was the barrier, not her lack in ability.

TIP: The solutions shared to combat the common reasons for low confidence are to unhook (defuse), be more self-accepting and self-encouraging, make room for the feeling, practice skills and gain experience, while diligently following the confidence cycle of applying, assessing and modifying confidence skills as needed.

Goals and Values

The book gives in-depth look at goals and values. It is continuously emphasized that values-based decisions are key to success and well-being. Whether in love, work, health or play, the importance we place on our underlying values determines the strength and stamina with which we will pursue our goals such as confidence in social situations. If we want to rise above our nervous interaction to honor our value of being "friendly and warm to others," we will be committed to interacting with others in this manner regardless of how we feel. This will in turn build confidence in a social context.

Key Takeaway: Goals are determined by values.

The discussion on personal values reminds us of the truth that our values are permanently in the background. Goals are determined by values and motivation to achieve those goals will be driven by the values we embody. Setting goals which contradict our values will result in frustration, failure and confusion about where we went wrong. Values are who we were meant to be and what we want the result to look like, so committed action helps us get to where we truly belong—the confident actions, for example.

Key Takeaway: Values are permanent.

Reiterating the fixed nature of our value system, Rule 5 states a need to hold values lightly (because they will never truly leave us) but to try with all our might to live them out and honor them. Satisfaction in life and confidence to be who we are depend on how well we live out our values because values are the measuring line for true success in our individual journeys.

Key Takeaway: Values are the main source of motivation for achieving difficult or elusive goals.

When the going gets tough, we fall back on our values: our reason for being. When a goal stands alone from our value system, it will fall at the first sign of struggle or weakness. Values-based goals, however, rely on self-starting stamina and an enduring motivation.

Key Takeaway: Living by your values is instant success.

As per Rule 6, living by your values is the very definition of success. If we live with integrity, we are happy. If we achieve goals which honor our value system, we are satisfied and proud to be there.

Taking into account the world's version of success, it is easy to see where we become disillusioned. The winner-loser mentality is detrimental to our happiness because with a goal-focused life" we are simply a winner who succeeds until we are a loser who fails—there is no middle ground. "*It creates a desperate need to achieve, fueled by the fear of becoming a loser or a failure. This in turn leads to chronic stress, performance anxiety, or burnout*" (Harris, Ch. 7).

Emotional Intelligence

Key Takeaway: Beliefs and associations from lifelong habits and ingrained childhood messages are hard to crack.

Stemming from the values, experiences and patterns learned since early childhood, our minds are capable of coming up with endless reasons why things are so. Minds can criticize, overanalyze, tell us a thousand ways we should not or cannot do something; judge, rank, and grade our handiwork or ideas; and predict unfavorable outcomes for anything we churn out. Harris refers to this as "reason-giving."

We are encouraged to think critically about the information and sensory inputs around us, not to simply accept face value based on our own proclivities. A scientific approach is to question, compare and probe information before allowing it to internalize (or fuse) with our worldviews. Origin is everything.

TIP: A scientific approach is to question, compare and probe information before allowing it to internalize (or fuse) with our worldviews. Origin is everything.

Key Takeaway: Making room for difficult feelings and thoughts creates opportunities to grow

Experiential avoidance is the way we choose comfort in short term gains rather than discomfort in pursuit of real long-term fulfillment. Instead of contentment, we choose insta gratification and the path of least resistance. Instead of commitment to honoring our values-based goal, we choose an unworkable alternative and settle for less.

Once we are mindful of these tendencies, we can push through the momentary discomfort and reach the precipice of real joy and lasting satisfaction. Learning to deal with difficult feelings and thoughts makes way for greatness; success becomes a probability.

TIP: The defusion technique to "notice it, name it and then neutralize it" helps us prepare for this expansion. The "Leaves on a Stream" exercise is where we notice the thought, name it or give it an innocuous title, and then imagine it floating past us like a leaf on a stream, effectively neutralizing its effect on us.

Fear

Chapter 3 approaches the complexities of fear, reminding readers of its prominence in the search for confidence. As it turns out, fear and confidence are not mutually exclusive. Bizarre as it sounds, it is possible to be afraid and confident at the same time.

"But there's no way to expand your comfort zone without stepping out of it—and the moment you take that step, fear is going to show up" (Harris, Ch. 3).

Key Takeaway: Fear is here to stay as a vital part of survival and performance.

Human nature is geared toward survival at all costs. The mind is wired to react for our preservation and protection in the classic fight-flight-or-freeze response mentioned in the cognitive-behavioral therapy field. Fear is a built-in survival tool, giving us the push to avoid danger and live another day. Sometimes it is part of the relentless inner 'radio' voice— *"little fascist dictator inside your head, always demanding more."*

TIP: Don't fight it, neutralize it. We do this by using the defusion techniques, like singing it in a silly voice or hearing it as a nursery rhyme.

Key Takeaway: Fear is your ally.

The four myths of fear addressed in the book are: "fear is a sign of weakness; fear impairs performance; fear holds you back; and confidence is the absence of fear" (Harris, Ch. 3).

Relating fear to the taming of a wild stallion, the ABC formula for "fear-whispering" (to transform your relationship with your fear into a positive partnership) is to allow it, to befriend it and then to channel it.

TIP: Allow it to be in your mind without trying to control it. Notice it, name it then neutralize it. Then be 'friendly' towards it. "Welcome fear, thanks fear" and channel it into energy for achieving the task you have set with confidence.

Key Takeaway: The problem is FEAR. The solution is DARE.

FEAR is:

Fusion with unhelpful thoughts and feelings,

Excessive goals and expectations,

Avoidance of discomfort rather than pursuit of long-term success, and

Remoteness from values.

Its antidote is DARE:

Defusion,

Acceptance of discomfort,

Realistic goals, and

Embracing values.

MOTIVATION

Key Takeaway: Lack of motivation is lack of commitment

Motivation is values-based, especially when the going gets rough. Similar to the confidence gap, the motivation gap is where we tend to 'wait until we feel motivated' before committing to any action. This approach looks at motivation as a feeling, a sensation that moves us. It is a trap and can be counteracted by adjusting RULE 1 to read, "the actions of motivation come first, the feelings of motivation come later."

Key Takeaway: Failure is not a reason for complacency

Successful people fail. They also try again, and again, and again, until they succeed. Their commitment is to values-based living, not to individual goals.

The tips for rebounding from failure include: 'unhooking' (defusing), making space for it to exist in your reality without trying to avoid it, being kind to yourself, appreciating the positives, finding useful information to take to heart and taking a stand for what you truly believe is right. In the end, failure makes us stronger, wiser and better.

But we do have some choice about the type of pain we experience. We can choose the pain of stagnation, or we can choose the pain of growth" (Harris, Ch. 18).

Genuine Confidence

Harris refers to a boost of self-esteem as a poor indicator of confidence. It should not be dependent on circumstances or feelings or experiences, although all of this works together for developing the skills to act with confidence. Genuine confidence is the ability to rely on yourself, to trust yourself with mindful attention to every moment, in any area of life, regardless of thoughts, feelings or situations: a complex but meaningful encouragement for those stuck in the confidence gap.

Key Takeaway: The actions of confidence precede the feelings, which may or may not appear later.

The confidence gap, or how reality falls short of expectation, is affected by the popular notion that possessing confidence is the first step towards success or peak performance. This is a myth; it results in inaction, complacency and disappointment as people wait for the confidence to proceed.

Repeated throughout the narrative is the first rule of the confidence game:

"RULE 1: The actions of confidence come first, the feelings of confidence come later"

Acting with commitment in spite of fear is an example of where the 'feeling' of confidence is missing, but where action is still possible. It is also beneficial to remember you have more control over your actions than over your feelings.

Key Takeaway: Genuine confidence will change you.

The first exercise in the 'Life-Change List' asks a variety of poignant questions about your vision and hope for confident living. Following basic cognitive-behavioral therapy techniques and putting the ball in your court, it asks for details on how your life would be different with unlimited confidence.

Would you behave, walk, or talk differently? How would your relationships and performance change? How would you change the way you see yourself, others and your body? It also touches on self-talk, prohibition, values and goals and impact upon the world. Checking off the Life-Change List becomes a reality, as you realize you can do a lot of these things by making a commitment to action even without the 'feeling' of confidence.

EDITORIAL REVIEW

"Many people are completely lost in something I call "the confidence gap." It's that place we get stuck when fear gets in the way of our dreams and ambitions... 'Until I feel more confident'" (Harris, Ch. 1).

A book about how to improve confidence is hardly a novel idea in our self-help culture, but readers may find a slightly unique approach in *The Confidence Gap*. This is the bottom line: everyone dreams of possessing absolute confidence, but most people approach it like a lucky draw rather than a guarantee. In Harris' world, confidence lies well within our grasp and he presents a persuasive argument and a myriad of tools to this end.

Harris seems to have the formula for a bestseller meticulously planned out: a conversational tone, a casual venturing into meaningful and controversial topics, a dash of pop culture references, celebrity name-dropping, cliché examples of 'known truths,' and just enough admission of his personal shortcomings to reassure readers they are not alone. Despite this recognizable approach and some obvious repetition, the read feels neither superficial nor derelict. To the contrary, evokes a healthy dose of self-reflection and relatable application.

Acceptance and Commitment Training (or ACT, pronounced as the noun "to act," not spelled out A-C-T) is the order of the day. ACT's premises are foundational to everything which discussed, presented or analyzed in the book. ACT is made both accessible and attractive, seeking to pinpoint core personal values at the root of committed action, lasting motivation, and curious inspiration without the psycho-babble. There is a sensible truth behind the explanatory phrases and acronyms of ACT with abundant flexibility to fit any mold or personality.

The focus is on confidence, or lack thereof, and why our reality is sometimes caught in a disappointing 'gap,' far off the mark of rosy expectations. The methodology promises a life of unshackled confidence at the end of the struggle. It does not shy away from fear or discomfort, acknowledging these challenges as another part of the journey towards confident contentment.

Achieving success means realizing dreams, opening up a new perspective and being true to the values which drive it all. As the story unfolds, it is easy to see how these tools may be applied not only in the search for confidence, but in other areas, too.

The insightful discussion zooms through Harris' ten rules of confidence, revealing how and why our minds inevitably work against us in the game of confidence. Easy-to-follow commentaries and mindfulness tools are provided throughout the light-hearted exchange. It appears that diligent practice and "committed action" may indeed result in a curious expectancy, limitless motivation, the acceptance (not the eradication) of fear, the development of self-awareness and ultimately, the benefits of genuine confidence.

Finally, equipped with tools to handle the incessant chatter of an apparently pessimistic inner voice common to all mankind, by the end of Part 5 it is a wonder we ever lacked confidence in the first place. Or it will be once our committed lifetime of practice climaxes in a confident life of "success and fulfillment."

BACKGROUND ON AUTHOR

Russ Harris, a British citizen now residing in Australia, is a medical doctor who chose to move into psychology. Delving into a new vocation he is now a renowned psychotherapist, acclaimed stress-management expert and a published author. Passionate about Acceptance and Commitment Therapy (ACT) and its applications in health and well-being, he conducts executive coaching and training seminars for health professionals and members of the public alike.

His formal medical background created an interesting foundation from which to explore the health of mind and body. Considerably drawn to the effects on the human psyche over the years, he realized his interests and expertise lay more with the development of accessible mental health techniques than general medicine.

Convinced by the benefits of ACT, he has authored several books and self-help guides on the subject. A proponent of Psychological Flexibility, he avidly promotes this newly-discovered realm of human psychology as an excellent tool for performance enhancement, improved well-being and stress reduction. He even had a stint as a stand-up comedian before successfully going mainstream with his Psychological Flexibility workshops both nationally and internationally.

OTHER TITLES BY RUSS HARRIS

The Happiness Trap: How to Stop Struggling and Start Living: A Guide to ACT (2008)

ACT Made Simple: An Easy-To-Read Primer on Acceptance and Commitment Therapy (The New Harbinger Made Simple Series) (2009)

The Illustrated Happiness Trap: How to Stop Struggling and Start Living (2014)

ACT with Love: Stop Struggling, Reconcile Differences, and Strengthen Your Relationship with Acceptance and Commitment Therapy (2009)

The Reality Slap: Finding Peace and Fulfillment When Life Hurts (2012)

ACT Questions and Answers: A Practitioner's Guide to 150 Common Sticking Points in Acceptance and Commitment Therapy (2018)

Getting Unstuck in ACT: A Clinician's Guide to Overcoming Common Obstacles in Acceptance and Commitment Therapy (2013)

*** END OF BOOK SUMMARY***

*If you enjoyed this **ZIP Reads** publication, we encourage you to purchase a copy of the original book.*

We'd also love an honest review on Amazon.com!

Made in the USA
Monee, IL
30 March 2022